handing on the faith

Other *Handing on the Faith* titles:

When You Are a Single Parent

Jeanne Hunt

ST. ANTHONY MESSENGER PRESS

Cincinnati, Ohio

Scripture citations are taken from *New Revised Standard Version Bible,* copyright ©1989 by the Division of Christian Education of the National Council of the Churches of Christ in the U.S.A., and used by permission. All rights reserved.

Cover and interior illustrations by Julie Lonneman

Cover and book design by Constance Wolfer

Library of Congress Cataloging-in-Publication Data

Hunt, Jeanne.
 When you are a single parent /c Jeanne Hunt.
    p. cm. — (Handing on the faith)
  ISBN 0-86716-519-7 (pbk.)
 1. Single parents—Religious life. 2. Parenting—Religious aspects—Catholic Church. 3. Single parents—Prayer-books and devotions—English. 4. Catholic Church—Prayer-books and devotions—English. I. Title. II. Series.
  BX2352 .H86 2003
  248.8'45—dc21

                              2002155752

ISBN 0-86716-519-7

Copyright ©2003, Jeanne Hunt
All rights reserved.

Published by St. Anthony Messenger Press
www.AmericanCatholic.org
Printed in the U.S.A.

Contents

Introduction

Living life as a parent is a blessed vocation. While it all begins with a twosome, some of us by choice or circumstances find ourselves parenting alone. Though the situation is not unique in our society, the challenges of going it alone demand unique skills. "Alone again, naturally" are lyrics which strike a chord in the heart of every single parent. Regrouping after a death or divorce, having a child without having a partner or enduring a long separation from your spouse can leave you feeling like you have strayed from the path, living a family lifestyle that is outside of God's plan. Our culture would have us believe that our lives should be according to some planning book that assumes we will always have control over our choices. But that is not the way God does things. God's plan is unique for each of us and for each of our families. Once you can accept that truth and embrace your vocation as a single parent, the grace begins to soak into your family life. There is no best way to be family. God has many options for holiness.

Nothing Is Impossible with God

Embrace your state of life with trust in God's care. Parenting, under any circumstances, is an overwhelming job; it is not wrong to think that parenting alone is impossible. Fortunately, you are not alone. When you allow the Divine Partner to join you, remarkable things begin to happen. Accept that God will give you the means, the inspiration and the energy to live out your vocation. Act on this belief and life moves forward with purpose and growth begins. Initially, it is a matter of attitude and belief. Resolve to build your family life on the firm foundation of faith.

The Example of the Holy Family

God did not make life easy on the woman who gave that complete "yes." When Mary consented to be the mother of Jesus, she was very young, betrothed, but not married, and living in a world where women who committed adultery (as her community must have imagined she did) were stoned to death. She may very well have expected that her future husband would not be willing to marry her; that her family and friends would abandon her; that, perhaps, her community would sentence her to death. Still, in one moment, she committed her life to fulfilling the role God placed before her. There is no better model for the single parent. Each day will present a thousand moments in which you must renew your commitment to being the mother or father God created you to be. You will never know what the result of your actions will be—only God knows that. Seek God's guidance and trust that whatever you do for love of God and family will bear the fruit of faith and love.

Have the Courage to Accept Your Situation

The way to begin is to summon all your courage and just...begin. Look at your family, your circumstances, your pain and your blessings and accept all of it as your very real world. You cannot wish any of it away. You can start to change it for the better, but first you must see your circumstances without denial. Sometimes you have to step back and look at the harsh reality of who you are and what happened to you with a graced-filled resignation. You simply cannot make it other than it is.

The exercise of taking stock of our situation is primary to healing and growth. Elise, a divorced mother of four, spent two full years denying that her husband's leaving had changed her life at all. Everyday she pretended he was just "out of town" for a while. But she was earning half the salary they had shared, her house was falling into disrepair and her boys struggled without their father's presence. Finally, in a moment of desperation she sat with a counselor and cried out her rage and saw her life with new eyes: "It was the most freeing experience of my life. Once I faced my sorry state and decided to find the courage to *be* again, everything turned around."

Begin by drawing deep within and deciding that you are going to trust God. Trusting God is not just a sweet platitude. It means believing beyond logical proof that somehow all will be well. The faith-filled person has access to a unique virtue called hope. It is time to take it from the storeroom of your religious training, shake it out and put it on like a garment. Hope means believing that you are in the constant care of a loving God who gives you all you need to abide in life. It is an innate confidence that you need not worry about "what you are to eat and what you are to drink" (Luke 12:29) because God will care for you. When you consciously make the choice to live in that kind of radical hope, your life takes on an ease that Saint Paul calls the "peace that surpasses all understanding." It doesn't mean we can sit back and glide through life. It means that God will provide answers, means and help as we actively work to live well. Hope is a childlike trust that the Creator loves us and will never abandon us.

The Lord is near. Do not worry about anything, but in everything by prayer and supplication with thanksgiving let your requests be made known to God. And the peace of God, which surpasses all understanding, will guard your hearts and your minds in Christ Jesus. (Philippians 4:5–7)

Use a Network of Support

O nce you can rise above the issue that put you in the single-family category, it is time to regroup and establish a framework of support. Phyllis, who became a single mother after the death of her husband, believes that the key to her success was, "Extend, extend, extend." She looked to her mother, sisters and brother to be involved in her life as much as possible. She extended the circle beyond family to include other families from her son's school and her longtime friends. This larger group offered advice, companionship and support because she asked for it. The potential island of an only child with his mom became an open house filled with neighbors, family and friends who became involved. Extend your circle of family members and friends. Children (and parents!) need loved ones to share Little League games, Christmas suppers, vacations at the beach and even the worries of adolescent rebellion. Have the courage and humility to ask for help.

Connecting with the Church

An indispensable part of this extended network is a firm connection with your faith community. Even if your relationship with the local parish has been distant, it is essential to reconnect. The spiritual dimension is crucial to inner stability. Worshipping as a family is not negotiable. This may mean starting from scratch and learning (or relearning) the faith with your children. It is not unusual to put the spiritual life on hold when starting a family—there are so many responsibilities clamoring for our attention that we ask God to wait. And God does wait. But we cannot wait for long; we begin to feel a void in our depths, when we most need to find extra strength. Our sense of life's meaning becomes distorted and our moral stamina fails to develop. We need a spiritual foundation on which to establish family life, a foundation that will support us and our children.

If you have been away from church, begin to attend Sunday Mass. Receive the Eucharist regularly, even daily if possible. This is our spiritual food. Look for an area of ministry in your church that you would enjoy. Carmen, a single mom, joined the Young Mother's group in her parish. She said, "At first I felt awkward because I was the only mom without a partner. I hung in there and pretty soon these women became my confidantes about daily life with a toddler. They showed me the God dimension in my life. I am not a 'churchy' person, but now I actually am praying with my little girl. It makes all the difference in the world."

Another important part of fostering the faith connection within your family is to get your children involved in parish groups. So many parishes have children's ministries and youth groups that can bring the experience of faith into an age-appropriate understanding. Peer-group support is an excellent way to allow children to share their faith. Whether it's summer Bible school, Sunday children's liturgy or the parish school, take advantage of your church's outreach to children.

A Network of Care

Finally, look for other single-parent families in the church and school with whom to network. These relationships become invaluable as we look for understanding and support in those situations that normally require a two-parent effort. Sharing responsibilities like carpools, child care and housework will make life a little easier for everyone—not to mention sharing the burden of going it alone.

These single parents can also offer great advice on house maintenance, budgets and child discipline. Learning to cook or to replace window screens can be bonuses in this network of single-parent connections. You may even want to consider joining a support group that is already providing this network. Whatever direction you choose, it is primary that you work with others who understand what it takes to live the single-parent vocation with success and happiness.

For Reflection and Discussion

• *Make a list of family members and friends whom you need and value. Resolve to see them more often and ask for their help when necessary.*

• *Join your parish church and attend Sunday Mass.*

• *Volunteer for some activity at your parish.*

• *Get your child(ren) involved in a parish children's group.*

• *Make a list of single-parent families in your community. Begin to look for a way to network with them.*

For as in one body we have many members, and not all the members have the same function, so we, who are many, are one body in Christ, and individually we are members one of another. We have gifts that differ according to the grace given to us.... [L]ove one another with mutual affection; outdo one another in showing honor.... Rejoice in hope, be patient in suffering, persevere in prayer. (Romans 12:4–6, 10, 12)

THE COURAGE TO ASK

Holy Spirit,
Give me the courage to reach out.
Help me to see that I am not alone.
The circle of your love surrounds me.

That circle is filled with so many others
That you wish to bring to me,
To teach, work, laugh, care, cry,
And a thousand other little graces
That are meant for me and my children
If I just have the courage to ask.

Amen.

Set Limits

Family rules become the framework of expectations for what is acceptable in your family. Rules and expectations are also the framework of God's loving care within the family structure. Respecting one another and keeping a code of family rules creates an atmosphere of mutual love that mirrors God's love. However, when we parent alone, there is no one to back us up on discipline decisions. It becomes very important to create a family rules system in which the family unit comes to a common understanding of the rules and the consequences for breaking them. We must not fail to communicate the boundaries; everyone must know the rules that define conduct in our family.

Children owe their parents respect, gratitude, just obedience, and assistance. Filial respect fosters harmony in all of family life. (*Catechism of the Catholic Church*, #2251)

Teaching our children that we live by a code of ethics found in the Gospel is an important part of their formation. Obedience remains a struggle throughout our lives. The world preaches a "do your own thing" gospel without regard for the needs of others. The church teaches us to honor our parents. When families abide by common rules and respect parental authority, harmony begins and the stress of arguing through every decision is alleviated. The easiest way to establish a foundation of these moral principles is to spend time teaching your child the most basic laws of God. When we live the Ten Commandments and the Golden Rule within our families, we develop a moral fiber that remains all our lives. Take time to point out to your child when something is morally wrong. When watching television or listening to music, point out when immoral behavior is presented and explain why it is wrong. These basic faith moments will guide your child to moral maturity.

Creating the family rules is an ongoing process. Initially, gather with everyone and write down some basic rules that are important to you. Rules like "Call if you will be late" or "Homework is always finished before supper" are some examples. Gather for a family meeting each month. A Sunday evening after dinner is an ideal time for this gathering. At these meetings, anyone can bring up the need to change, modify or add a new family rule. It's important to have general consensus on these rules, and established consequences for breaking them. For example, a child who comes home after curfew without a phone call can expect to stay home the next weekend. Remember to keep a little flexibility in your system, too. You may outgrow a rule as the children mature, or a family situation—losing a job or taking on a new responsibility—may change the way the rule needs to be used. Even when children are too young to participate meaningfully in these discussions, it is important to establish patterns of collaborations by letting them offer their two-cents' worth. Keep the doors of communication open and do not write your rules in stone.

Honor the Consequences

Once the rules are in place, be consistent in their practice. Even when you are willing to understand the reason (or excuse) for breaking the rules, you must enforce the consequences. Rob, a divorced father of three teenage girls, struggles with being too lenient. He wants to give in to his girls when they push him. When he caught his fourteen-year-old daughter Bridget with cigarettes, she told him they belonged to her friend and, therefore, there should be no punishment. Rob said, "I knew we had reached a point where I could not back down. We had agreed that having alcohol and cigarettes meant a week's grounding. So I stuck to my guns. After that, Bridget knew that there was no way she could talk around breaking the rules." Of course, it is often easier to avoid the hassle of enforcing consequences for breaking the rules, but good parenting is never easy. In the long run, enforcing the rules will ensure that children respect the limits, resulting in a healthier and happier life for everyone.

Red-Alert Situations

After you have created the boundaries and set the example of sticking to the consequences, what can we do when things get out of hand? There are those times when you need support in dealing with a more serious situation. Perhaps, a toddler will not go to her day care without a panic attack, or your grade-school child has taken a nosedive academically, or a teenager is angry and refusing to obey the family rules at all. Where do you go with these situations? It is imperative that you learn to recognize when you need help.

There will be times when you cannot be all things to your children. It is at these times that you feel most alone—who else could possibly understand the complex situation, or share your feelings? When you feel the need for support, ask for help. Do not let the situation escalate until it is out of control. Learn to rely on family members, pastors, teachers, psychologists and friends to step in and work with you to guide and correct when it is beyond you. Recognize that you cannot be everywhere. Joan's fifteen-year-old son was constantly sneaking out at night after the household had gone to bed. She would go to bed exhausted and wake up at 2 A.M. to check on the children, only to find Joe missing and a rope hanging from his bedroom window to the ground outside. After repeatedly discussing it with him and punishing him,

Joan was at her wits' end. She mentioned the problem to her older brother who offered to help. The next Friday night, her brother patiently waited beneath the window for the rope to appear. Sure enough, about 11:15 Joe shimmied down the side of the house—only to be met by Uncle Tom. What followed was the first in a series of heart-to-heart talks between a defiant young man and an uncle who became a confidant in the place of an absentee dad. Joe needed a father figure in his life. Joan had the grace to invite her brother into the situation and do what she could never do for her son.

For Reflection and Discussion

- *Make a list of important family rules and the consequences for breaking the rule. Ask other family members to do the same.*

- *Schedule your first Family Meeting to create the "Family Rules."*

- *Post a list of the rules on the refrigerator, bulletin board or some central location.*

- *Anticipate difficult family situations when you will need help. Write down the names of people whose strengths will complement your own when a difficult situation arises.*

The law of the Lord is perfect, reviving the soul; The decrees of the Lord are sure, making wise the simple. (Psalm 19:7–8)

Rooted in Love

Divine Keeper,
How do we make sense of your ways?
Teach us to take what we know about a good life,
And turn it into our good life.
Help us to sort out what is important
And learn how to uphold it.
Give us the strength to stick to our decisions
Especially when giving in would be so much easier.
Help us remember that your law is rooted in love,
And our rules must be rooted in that same love.

Amen.

Create a Balance

Organizing the Time Pie

The daily life of a single parent is a case history in overload. Being Mom and Dad, coach and housekeeper, nurse and cook and a hundred other occupations will wear you very thin. It is vital that you create time every day for work, relaxation and a little planned prayer time. As you begin to model this you will lead your children into this habit as well. Begin to look at the day with an eye for balance.

Resentment at not "having one minute to myself" finally sent Patricia to the edge. She wondered how other folks found time to enjoy life with all the responsibilities of single parenting. That's when she learned that a little time management works as well at home as it does at work. Now, each evening Patricia makes a list of what she needs to do the next day. The first item on her daily list is always prayer time. She always includes one rest or creative activity for herself, like "watch my favorite TV program" or "go for a walk after supper." Then she fills the list with all the work to be done in order of importance. She works her way down the list throughout the day. Whatever doesn't get done on today's list gets priority on tomorrow's list. Every night she spends a little time in prayer making the next day's list. This simple method has passed the test of time in Patricia's house, and she says she no longer resents her schedule because she "and God" have a daily plan.

Keep in mind that children, too, need structure and organization in their days and weeks. Praying as a family to discern how to manage commitments and obligations can be an important step in allowing God's presence into your family schedules. When children learn to pray with you about their plans, they will receive the added bonus of confidence and peace about their choices.

Looking for Quality Time

One of the greatest areas of stress in the single parent family is a feeling of guilt for not spending more "quality time" with your children. While guilt is a famous Catholic commodity, the last thing an overwhelmed parent needs is guilt for being overwhelmed. Instead of having that perfect house and garden for your children to enjoy, put aside your chores and resolve to spend one hour of one-on-one time a week with each child. Let that hour be just the two of you doing whatever that child enjoys. Phyllis found herself attending rock concerts with her thirteen-year-old son. She later reflected, "The music was pure torture for me, but sharing that evening with Rick was music for my soul. I will always hold those concert nights as my most precious memories of Rick's young adolescent years." This individual time with your child builds a foundation of unconditional love and acceptance. The weekly time can be rather low-key, but once a month plan a "date" with your child. Your monthly date should be a priority on your schedule. Don't fall into the trap of putting it off. In fact, plan ahead by marking off the time and planning the activity at least a month in advance so that this special time never gets absorbed in day-to-day demands.

For Reflection and Discussion

• *Make a Time Pie. Get a paper plate and create slices of your time. Have as many slices as you need: work, sleep, housekeeping, shopping, community and school activities, leisure, prayer. Where do you need more time? What do you spend too much time doing? What would you like to do less?*

• *Resolve to create some quality time. Come up with a plan to make it happen.*

A false balance is an abomination to the LORD, but an accurate weight is his delight. (Proverbs 11:1)

TIMELY WISDOM

O Divine Time Keeper,
Where do the hours go?
I cannot seem to stretch myself far
    enough
And in the process I wear so thin.
Give me the wisdom to see
What is important to you.

Let me put aside anything that dilutes,
Or drains me from the genuine experience of my family.
Help me walk away from those things
That diminish your presence in our lives.
And help me choose to give my time
To those things that honor you.

Amen.

Plan Household Tasks

Coming Up with a Plan

Household chores and home maintenance are challenges for all families, more so those with single parents. Most single parents work full time outside the home and lack the extra cash to hire household help. But that does not mean you have to do all the housework yourself. At a family meeting, work out a cooperative housework schedule that involves everyone, taking into account the age and ability of each child. Make everyone responsible for cleaning their private space (bedrooms, bathrooms). Smaller children should have manageable tasks, such as putting the utensils away as an older sibling empties the dishwasher, or removing sticks and rocks from the lawn before Dad mows. Housework can be done whenever it fits best into your family schedule, but try to do a small portion every weekday so the house is always well-kept.

Weekends are the perfect time for maintenance work or seasonal cleaning jobs. Carpet cleaning, gutter cleaning or repairing a door can teach the whole family how to use a shampooer, a ladder and a screwdriver. However, don't take on work that is well beyond your skills. You have enough frustration and stress. Sometimes the wise thing to do is to save up the money to hire a professional to do a sidewalk repair or plumbing job. If money is lacking, perhaps you could swap jobs with someone else: Make a family dinner in exchange for a minor plumbing task, for example. Use good judgment and place the safety and happiness of your family before all other concerns.

The final element of your weekly plan should include daily family prayer. If you want your children to know how to share their lives with God, you must model it. This prayer time could be at the end of the day when you tuck your little ones into bed, before you leave in the morning for school and work or whenever it works best for your family. As your family changes, the time and place may change, but never give it up.

The Christian family is a communion of persons.... It is called to partake of the prayer and sacrifice of Christ. Daily prayer and the reading of the Word of God strengthen it in charity. (*Catechism of the Catholic Church*, #2205)

Prayer will be the glue that holds your family together. Prayer will be the touchstone for feelings and needs that have no other place to be spoken. The Holy Spirit will inspire the most tongue-tied children to speak their heart's needs in a circle of prayer.

For Reflection and Discussion

• *Create a working plan to maintain your home.*

• *List some chores that you can afford to hire out. Start a savings account to handle these repairs.*

• *List jobs your children can do. Stop doing them yourself and teach the children to do them.*

I know the plans I have for you, says the LORD, plans for your welfare and not for harm, to give you a future with hope. (Jeremiah 29:11)

WHO'S IN CHARGE HERE?

O God,
I wish you were in charge of my life!
How simple it could be
If I could just get up every morning
And take orders from you!
You are in charge,
I have just forgotten to listen to your directions.

Come to me, Good Shepherd,
And lead our family into the ways of heaven.
Teach us to work together,
And not to worry about all the details.
You have told us not to be anxious about the little things
So, Lord, we will try to trust you a little more with our lives.
Shepherd us, Lord.

Amen.

Establish Priorities

The Superman Syndrome

Saint Augustine tells us that our biggest problems come from trying to do too much good. One of the greatest sources of sin is having too many good things from which to choose. All the things on our "To Do List" are in themselves worthwhile, but we must decide what is most important and put aside everything else. Saint Augustine says, "You cannot give what you do not have." This means that we must be honest with ourselves and learn our limits. It is remarkably freeing to say you cannot do something and not feel guilty about it. We all have the mistaken impression that we are the saviors of the world. Releasing that job to the One who can do it allows us to do a few things very well and leave the rest to him.

Priorities

Begin to take time out to really think about what is important to you. Establishing a priority list is the first step to creating a family life that is full of growth and well-being. Perhaps being a part of a child's sport activities is high on your list while keeping up with the yard work is a nagging chore. Until you actually begin to list these priorities, it might never occur to you to eliminate as much gardening as possible so that you would have the time to be at your child's games. Rob is a single parent who began to take apart his week and look at what he was spending his time doing and compare that to what he wanted to do with his time. This exercise led Rob to hire a cleaning service for his home twice a month so that his weekends were free to play golf with his teenage son, Jason. Not only did his house stay cleaner, but he and Jason finally had that quality time together. When you establish what is important to your family and begin working toward making these things happen, the frustrations of a fractured life begin to dissolve and you begin to live a new life with a guided purpose.

Time Out to Think and Pray

Getting it all together can seem overwhelming to the hassled single parent: We barely have time to survive the day, much less actually think about what we want and need to do. There is a deep sense of hopeless fatigue that plagues us. Sometimes even the important and necessary things are too much for us. What can we do to get back on track and live a "together" family life? First of all, we must take some time out to really think things through. Perhaps you could schedule a retreat at a local spiritual center or clear a Sunday afternoon for yourself and spend some quiet time alone with God and a notebook. Pray first, asking the Holy Spirit to inspire your thoughts. Honestly ask yourself what would make your home life better. What should you eliminate? What things are important but simply impossible to fit into your schedule? What can you do to accomplish those necessary priorities?

Healthy, Wealthy and Wise

Remember that you cannot be Superman or Wonder Woman. Trying to fulfill unrealistic expectations will only cause frustration and burnout. Killing the golden goose will not make anyone richer. You cannot compromise your own health and well-being in the pursuit of some superhuman ideal. Keeping your body well, eating healthy foods and getting enough sleep can be the difference between failure and making your life run like a well-oiled machine. If you break down, the whole system stops. There is no one to pick up the slack. Keeping yourself healthy must be your first priority.

The basic disciplines of a healthy lifestyle are not overwhelming and for most of us requires only minor adjustments in the way we live. Here are some of the basics:

Know how much sleep you need and get it, every night. Don't be tempted to skimp—it will catch up with you later. If your schedule makes a good night's sleep impossible, get rest when you can or even take a nap.

Eat a healthy diet. Plan your menus and keep healthy foods in stock so you won't be tempted to hit the fast-food drive-through on the way home from work.

Have an exercise routine. At least three times a week plan to walk, work out or get some physical exercise.

Besides keeping your body working well, exercise is a great stress reliever.

Have routine medical and dental checkups. Prevention is the key to staying healthy. A good relationship with a caring doctor will be one of those support systems that can keep you feeling good about yourself.

It is difficult for many single parents to accept the need for self-care. Even if you do not see their importance now, think of these steps as setting a valuable example for your children. As your health and outlook improve, you will have more reasons to continue.

For Reflection and Discussion

• *Buy a notebook and decide to use it once a month to reflect on the state of your family. Make a date with the Holy Spirit to pray and reflect with your notebook.*

• *In the family notebook, make a list of the priorities for your family. Plan to regularly revisit the notebook to make changes.*

• *Begin to take care of your health as if you are caring for someone you love very much, someone your children love and depend upon.*

Come to me, all you that are weary and are carrying heavy burdens, and I will give you rest. Take my yoke upon you, and learn from me; for I am gentle and humble in heart, and you will find rest for your souls. (Matthew 11:28–29)

DOING IT ALL

Lord, somehow I have slipped into
    the savior mode.
Quite by accident, I decided that I
    could do it all.
I am the savior of my world.
I didn't really mean to walk away from you,
But the world encourages me to believe
That I am a super hero,
Master of my fate,
Capable of doing everything that I set my mind to.
But, Lord, I remember that you have the claim to the title
    "Savior."
You lifted my burdens high on a cross,
So that I don't need to stand alone,
I can stand with you.
Take my hand, gentle Savior,
And lead me on the path of peace.
I need you.
Help me.

Amen.

Celebrate Family Moments

Savoring Life

The art of savoring life is the work of a lifetime. For single-parent families this ability is especially elusive. Learn to appreciate the holy moments literally woven throughout the day: the funny things your three-year-old says, the late-night pizza supper with a house full of teenagers, the unexpected hug. Begin to do this for yourself and teach your family to do it; family life will seem slower and more blessed. One of the greatest legacies you can pass on to your children is the art of enjoying life.

Celebrating the Everyday Feasts

Celebrate the ordinary. Throughout the year there are hundreds of celebrating moments: a six-year-old losing a first tooth, the dog's birthday, the first day of spring and many others. Begin to take advantage of these occasions as moments of grace. Family life is sacred and worth celebrating.

Terry is a mom whose husband is in the Navy so, for at least six months of the year, she is the sole parent in their family. She loves to create special occasions when her husband is at sea. One evening she had a Backward Supper. Everyone wore their clothes backward, dessert was served first and they ended with an appetizer. Terry reflected after the event, "Our spirits were so low that I had to do something. John still had four more weeks at sea and I wondered where I would find the energy and patience to endure. The Backward Supper was wonderful. Our laughter eased the tension and gave us all a little break from the long wait for Dad to come home."

Seasonal feasts like Valentine's Day, St. Patrick's Day, or the Fourth of July, can also be occasions of celebrating. Make time to do a little something special on these days. Family rituals to honor the theme of a special day tell our children that savoring life is an important part of their spirituality. Making homemade cards on Valentine's Day, putting green food coloring in the milk on Saint Patrick's day, watching a community parade on the Fourth of July take little money and give us a chance to enjoy the fun of just being family. This celebrating spirit gives balance to the serious work and responsibility of single parents, balance that is so important in creating good family life. Children and parents need to experience work and play in equal measure.

The Family Vacation

Making time for some R & R is an important ingredient of a healthy family. When Genesis tells us that God rested on the seventh day, we are supposed to take notice that God wishes us to take time out to rest from our work. When you are giving a hundred percent to the financial well-being of your family, you deserve a little time to enjoy yourself and restore your spirit for the ongoing struggle of being alone in that effort. Vacations are not a luxury to the single parent. They are a necessity. These times out from the daily grind bring the family together to just enjoy each other without any expectations. Spiritual balance requires effort and determination. It is easy to say no to a vacation break. But remember you are the beloved of God. How do you treat those you love? Well, God wants to give you the same care. Caring for yourself as the beloved of God means knowing when it is time to take that break from your work and be restored.

Vacations need not be expensive or lengthy. In fact the more creative you can get, the more fun the time will be. Perhaps a week at home visiting your hometown like a tourist will be the perfect time-out experience. Jim, a divorced dad, and his three boys spent a week on his cousins' farm learning a little about rural life. Jim said it was a great experience. They helped bring in the hay crop and it didn't cost a penny. Laura, a college student with a baby daughter, spent her spring break visiting a different state park every day with friends. Laura packed picnic lunches and the baby napped on a blanket while she visited with her friends. If you can afford a week at the beach or a cabin in the woods, don't feel guilty about doing it. Families that are stressed out week to week need to keep their balance by scheduling times of play. Your children's most cherished memories will come from the times you spent on these little breaks in the routine.

Whatever you plan to do, make sure it is something that is totally enjoyable to you. Even if you can only fit in a long weekend or day off every other month, these little breaks are refreshing to everyone. This is your time to enjoy life.

Empty Space

There is one final element to leisure time. This kind of leisure gives single-parent families a little empty space. It is a good idea to block off some time each month with nothing scheduled. Let your children decide what they would like to do with those hours. A Saturday afternoon at the mall, a movie night with a favorite video, a day hiking in the woods are all great spontaneous ways to "just be" together.

In the hectic pace of today's family life, these little blocks of empty time provide that necessary edge to cushion the demands of a pressing schedule. You will not be able to just let these time blocks happen. You must be determined to put aside these evenings or afternoons. The biggest temptation is to fill our spare time with work. Getting in a load of laundry or doing some bill-paying seems productive. Yet, the time spent doing something your child would enjoy is far more important in the long run. Craig, a widower with two young sons, started getting complaints from his neighbors because he didn't keep his lawn as well mowed as the rest of the neighborhood. When they complained to him, he simply said, "I'm raising sons, not grass." Craig's simple wisdom could apply to anyone raising children. Time with them is far more precious than keeping up with the neighbors' notions of home maintenance.

Plan to put aside the same time every month for this little break. You will begin to look forward to it. Carla and her two teenage daughters keep Sunday evenings as their sacred time to just sit around and talk. There is no agenda. They usually share a simple supper and talk about the things going on in their lives. Carla has a new sense of connectedness with the girls. She never had this time to hear what was going on in their lives until the three of them decided to make a promise to hold Sunday nights open for one another. It has really changed their lives.

For Reflection and Discussion

- *Plan a vacation for your family. Begin to put into place the resources it will take to have a vacation. Start to save, make a reservation or just inform work of your week away for R & R.*

- *Surprise your family with a little celebration on the next holiday. Make special plans to celebrate a birthday, a holiday or just a made-up occasion.*

- *Keep a list of moments in your week when you are able to stop and enjoy a moment of beauty. Keep the list in a spot where others can see it and add a few moments of their own.*

[T]he mother of Jesus said to him, "They have no wine." (John 2:3)

Fɪʟʟ ᴛʜᴇ Gʟᴀssᴇs!

Blessed Mother,
Teach me to relax and enjoy my life.
The words you spoke to your son at
    Cana
Resonate in my heart.
You knew that wine was important for the celebration,
You knew that the bride and groom needed the wedding
    party
To begin their marriage in joy.
Holy Mother, lead me into moments of playful grace.
Guide me into understanding the joy
Of celebrating life with my children.
Let me remember to stop and fill the glasses
With the wine of laughter,
The wine of rest,
And the wine of joyful play.

Amen.

Have a Spiritual Sanctuary

Celebrate the Sabbath

Honor Sundays as a holy day. Keeping holy the Sabbath seems to be passé in our culture. Too many families don't bother to go to church. Laundry and housework fill the afternoon, and shopping on Sunday is as common and accessible as any other day. In fact, there is little difference between Saturday and Sunday in our culture. But God calls us to put aside Sunday as sacred.

This means that Sunday Mass is not optional. We begin this day with the eucharistic liturgy. The whole day is spent in a prayerful mood. Families are called to relax and put their feet up on Sabbath. It is the day for a big family meal, leisure, family fun and time out from the workaday world. Celebrating the Sabbath with gusto will give your family a weekly opportunity to tend to their souls. Resting on the seventh day gives God a secure place in your family life. If your family cannot honor the traditional Sabbath because of work schedules, don't let that stop you. Begin your Sabbath on Saturday evening at sunset and resume the focus when you return home on Sunday evening. The important thing is to put aside a part of your week for rest in God's presence.

For many, this will be a radical change from our present Sunday agenda. You will have to find another time to get household chores and shopping done. Looking at Sunday as your one vacation day per week will transform your family. Sabbath becomes a time to grow together in faith and to celebrate God's life in your life. This subtle witness of faith will plant the seeds of a future spiritual life for your children. They will begin to see the Sabbath as a necessary part of life. When Sabbath life becomes natural to all of you, you will wonder how you lived without it. By honoring this holy day you allow space in your life for God.

God Lives Here

Another way to subtly say God is a part of your family life is to create a home with ritual signs and symbols of the faith. A crucifix should hang in the center of your home. This is the great sign of our redemption and will remind the family of his saving presence in the midst of all you do. A crucifix or picture of Jesus in the bedrooms is also a wonderful way to create a prayer focus for morning and night prayers. Other Catholic symbols, such as statues or pictures of saints and the Blessed Virgin Mary can add to the unspoken statement that the saints and angels are with us, too.

It is also a good idea to proclaim the church season. Advent wreaths and purple tablecloths, a nativity scene, crowns of thorns, paschal candles throughout the months displayed in a prominent spot like the coffee table or kitchen table make the holy seasons of the church year come home. This holy focus will lend to an atmosphere of home as a sanctuary. In the unspoken signs everyone begins to know that God is with us.

When children reach the teenage years, these signs do far more than talk. As young adults begin to distance themselves from the instructions of their parents and begin to "think for themselves," a simple candle or sacramental sign can speak for you. Cyndi hung a purple cloth and crown of thorns on the wall in back of the TV during Lent. She was delighted to see her girls staring at it off and on throughout Lent. They even began to talk about the thorns with her as an "awesome" sign of Christ's love. Visual reminders of faith can spark untold grace.

The Son Spot

The Hopi people have a wonderful custom that can bring holiness into every family. The Hopi believe that each person has a "sun spot." This is a place where you feel especially close to God. It could be the top of a sunny rock, a mountain stream or a windy bluff that looks down on the village. It is a spot where prayer comes easily and you simply feel wrapped in the arms of God. In our culture there is a wonderful adaptation of this belief: Look around your home for that one spot where prayer comes easily for you, perhaps the quiet corner of the living room where the window looks out on a majestic old pine tree, or the sunny spot in a bedroom that can warm your soul on the coldest of days.

Create this holy place in your home. It will be a

refuge for you from the hectic pace of the world. Your prayer corner can be a place to pray with your children and a place to send them when they need time out, alone with God. Make sure this place has a candle, a Bible and some sign of God's presence, perhaps a crucifix or favorite statue. As the liturgical seasons change, add a little reminder of the seasons, a little purple fabric in Lent, a bowl of water for Easter time, summer flowers in the Ordinary time of July. Let this place be the place where everyone can feel God's touch.

The Sacred in the Ordinary

Our homes are the domestic church. It is in the midst of family life that we discover God. Too often we miss the awesome touch of God's hand because we are racing from one moment to the next. Begin to slow the pace of your life. Allow God time to speak in the midst of your family. God is there at the dinner table. God is tucking in a toddler at bedtime and teaching her how to pray. God is sitting next to you late at night in your loneliness holding you close. We have to be still long enough to feel this Holy Presence.

Try to realize that your home and family are sacred. In fact as you begin to see God in your midst you will begin to see a change in the way you live. As you pause to pray before meals or talk about the homework or what's happening at work remember that God listens, too. Begin to ask yourself how Jesus would act in your situation. How would Jesus deal with my bills, my home repairs and my angry children? The answer to these questions is there. It just takes quiet and time to hear them.

Your home is a sacred place where God comes to just be with you and guide you through the hard work and stress of parenting. Invoke God's sacred presence in your home. Claim the space as holy. Bless it. See this sacredness in the ordinary things of life. As you begin to live with God, the ancient words "in him we live and move and have our being" (Acts 17:28) will be a part of your family life. It takes awareness and lots of reminders to invite God in. Living in this new way is radical and counter-cultural. It means that you make God and your spiritual life a priority. It means that your measure of what is right is based on the gospel. It means you must begin to reject the values of the world and live a new way. Holiness is not meant for a select few. It is meant for all of us. Some of the holiest people I know are doing exactly what you do and I do. The difference is they walk with God every minute.

For Reflection and Discussion

- *Begin to celebrate the Sabbath as a holy day: Go to Mass, have a big family meal and don't do any unnecessary work.*

- *Put a cross or other Catholic symbol in your home.*

- *Create a "Son Spot" in your home. Visit it regularly.*

- *Bless your home and choose to find the sacred in the ordinary.*

God blessed the seventh day and hallowed it, because on it God rested from all the work that he had done in creation. (Genesis 2:3)

A House Blessing

O Divine Housekeeper,
Bless our house.
Let it be a place of sanctuary,
A place where we can meet you in quiet corners.
Care for us within these walls.
Let our kitchen be a place where
Bread is broken and hearts are shared.
Let our rooms be filled with your sure presence.
May coming home always feel good.
Because in these walls there is harmony, peace and
    acceptance.
May your Sacred Heart be the heartbeat of this house.

Amen.

Maintain a Positive Energy

Compliments Are Priceless

Compliments are priceless moral boosters. One of the most tragic things in our world is that children grow up not knowing they are precious and loved. As a parent, your primary objective is to allow your child to know that they are precious in God's sight and truly loved. Sometimes it is difficult to give to our child the very thing that we lack. Everyone has moments of feeling unloved and rejected. It is important to create a loving, affirming atmosphere for your entire family. Each of us must come to know that we are unique, gifted, loved and priceless in God's sight and to one another. There is no better way to get that message across than to begin to say it.

Remember to offer a little honest praise every day. Being positive and honest about the good things your children (and you) do is the best way to counteract the pervasive negativity that plagues our society. Whining and complaining seem to be second nature to so many.

You need to establish a family life in which the focus is not on what is wrong, how we have failed or what we lack. Let the focus be on what is good about who we are and what we do. This very subtle difference will reap the fruit of inner assurance. All of you will see your lives as blessed and privileged simply by affirming the little things that are good in one another.

Honor the Unique Qualities of Your Family

Every family is different. We love different things, have different memories, come from different backgrounds. All these things are good and need to be cherished. By looking at who you are and where you came from as precious and worthwhile, you begin to feel and know that your family life is a gift you give to one another. Single-parent families need to know that their stories and their unique qualities are valuable.

Clare, a widow with four children, began writing the story of her husband's family and his story so that her children would have a memory of their father, who was killed in a car accident. She began asking friends who had known and grown up with Jeff to write a memory about him. Then she became so enthralled with this family story that she expanded it to include her own family roots. The result is a grand collection of pictures, stories and mementoes that give Clare's children a wonderful history lesson of who they are. Clare reflects, "In the beginning it was a grief exercise for me. Then it became much more. By telling and knowing our story we began to see God's hand in our lives. We began to see that we are something very special, the work of hundreds of people who came before us and whose story we keep deep in our hearts."

It is important to pass on the story of who you are with your children. Share favorite family stories. Keep photo albums, videos and journals of what your family is about. The end result is a strong heritage that affirms the beauty and honor that children need to see in their own family.

Love One Another Openly and Often

Loving one another means more than unconsciously believing that we love others. The key to living in love is to say so and do so! Show affection openly no matter how old your children are. A little hug or kiss on the cheek should be a part of the way we greet each other. If your children have grown up without outward displays of affection now is the time to begin. Simply ask them for a hug. You will be surprised how quickly giving affection becomes second nature.

Carol has been divorced for twelve years. She can often be seen with her son and three daughters at parish functions. The children never leave her without a good-bye hug and kiss. She tells of her pointed efforts to be affectionate: "Living without a partner can be a very sterile lifestyle. No one gets close to you physically and emotionally. I wanted the kids to not only have it in their heads that I love them, but also feel it with their hearts. At one of our family meetings we made a rule that we would always give an outward gesture of our love for one another whenever we come or go. At first it was difficult, embarrassing and awkward. Now, even fifteen-year-old Amy doesn't mind a public hug!" Family life is always a unique combination of style and manner. But every family should develop some special way to acknowledge that love binds us together. Working at the little rituals of love produces great benefits. Both parents and children begin to live as people who are loved.

For Reflection and Discussion

- *Try to offer one positive comment to those you live with each day this week.*

- *Tell a family memory or story with your children this week. Try to do this at least once a week.*

- *Begin a family story journal.*

- *Tell your family members you love them and begin to hug them a little more often.*

[L]ove one another with mutual affection; outdo one another in showing honor. (Romans 12:10)

ALONE AGAIN

Lord, sometimes the lonely walk
Without a partner is difficult.
I see other couples holding hands,
Sharing a meal, laughing together
And suddenly I feel lonely.
At these times let me remember your love,
Help me to know deep in my heart
That I am never alone as long as you are with me.
Teach me to spend more time with you,
To learn to acknowledge your love,
And to work at really loving myself.
Sometimes, I'm the last person I remember to love;
Let me love myself just the way you love me.
And, Lord, when the loneliness hits,
Hold me close to your heart and call me by name
And remind me that I am precious to you.

Amen.

Conclusion

There are no experts on how to live a perfect family life, much less any foolproof guidelines for living a holy, single-parent family life. One thing is sure: There are so many combinations of family that there can be no one way to do it right. It is up to you to look at your situation and create, with the help of God, a beautiful life. We cannot forget that even the Holy Family fell outside of what we think of as traditional. In the same way that God kept his own family, you can count on heavenly inspiration and grace. This creative effort is not yours alone. God leads you and wants you to do well. "I know the plans I have for you, says the LORD, plans for your welfare and not for harm" (Jeremiah 29:11). In the end all of us can rely on God to guide us in our vocation to be parents and disciples.

Look back over the pages of this book and remember what really struck you as important in your situation. Begin to respond to the exercises at the end of each chapter. Allow the grace of these exercises to penetrate the weaknesses in your life. Begin to give yourself credit for the marvelous journey you have already completed. Rather than look at the inadequacies in your life, see your family and home as successful in God's eyes. You will not be fooling yourself, for God is well pleased with your commitment and love. Just allow God to take you from here to wherever your dreams and God's awesome providence lead. You won't be sorry. Being alone, naturally, is a blessing in disguise.

Notes

Special Beach Day

by Donna Foley
illustrated by David Schimmell

PEARSON

Scott
Foresman

Editorial Offices: Glenview, Illinois • Parsippany, New Jersey • New York, New York
Sales Offices: Needham, Massachusetts • Duluth, Georgia • Glenview, Illinois
Coppell, Texas • Ontario, California • Mesa, Arizona

Every effort has been made to secure permission and provide appropriate credit for photographic material. The publisher deeply regrets any omission and pledges to correct errors called to its attention in subsequent editions.

Unless otherwise acknowledged, all photographs are the property of Scott Foresman, a division of Pearson Education.

Illustrations by David Schimmell

Photograph 12 B.G. Thomson/Photo Researchers, Inc.

ISBN: 0-328-13289-6

7 8 9 10 V010 14 13 12 11 10 09 08

Tony, Lisa, and Mom were having a special day at the beach.
"Let's make a sand castle," said Tony.

"Not yet," said Mom. "You need more sunscreen. The sun is strong today. Let's go find a place for our picnic."

Lisa pointed her finger at a tree. "We can find shade there," she said.

Tony clung to his mother's hand. Walking on the sand was hard.

"Look at the sky!" Tony said.
Dark clouds were rolling in.
"Those are rain clouds!" said Mom.

They heard a loud clap of thunder.
"Quick! Go to the car!" Mom said.
"The sky sounds angry!" Tony said.

"We are safer here in the car," Mom told Lisa and Tony. "It is not smart to be under tree branches when there is lightning."

Lisa was pressing her face against the car window. "I think the storm is cool!" she said.

Tony, Lisa, and Mom ate lunch. They waited for the storm to end.

"It stopped raining!" said Tony. "Can we go back to the beach?"

"Yes," Mom said. "But we need to stay on the sand. Lightning could still strike. The waves could be very high."

"The lifeguard says it's safe now, Mom," Lisa said. "There has not been thunder for thirty minutes. Let's swim!"
"Yes, let's swim!" said Tony.

Thunderstorms

Thunderstorms can happen very quickly. They are hard to predict. Thunderstorms can produce lightning, which can be dangerous.

To stay safe in a thunderstorm, seek shelter indoors. If you are inside, stay away from windows and don't use any electrical appliances or telephones.